WORKING STEAM
Stanier Jubilees

Geoff Rixon

Ian Allan PUBLISHING

Introduction

Sir William A. Stanier's 'Jubilee' class of three-cylinder '5XP' 4-6-0s were widely regarded as successful engines — just as well, considering 191 were built — but it was not all plain sailing (plain steaming?). They suffered some serious teething troubles in their infancy and gained a reputation for being somewhat temperamental. Yet the combination of the right locomotive and a competent crew could produce a fine performance: unassisted passage up steep inclines and speeds over 90mph (maximum recorded speed 97½mph).

The first of the class was No 5552, which entered service in May 1934, unnamed, as were the next 112 locomotives. Production was rapid — too rapid, considering this was a new, unproven design. But the London, Midland & Scottish Railway (LMS) was desperate to replace its ageing fleet of secondary express locomotives and thus found itself with a fleet of fine-looking modern engines which didn't work very well. After a couple of years or so, performance began to improve as modifications to superheaters and blastpipes started to produce results. Much more could probably have been done, particularly in the postwar years, to turn the 'Jubilees' into a truly outstanding class. There was some dabbling with double chimneys, but the advent of the BR Standards followed by impending dieselisation removed the incentive to develop the 'Jubilees' to their full potential.

Front cover: No 45649 *Hawkins* of Kentish Town shed (14B) works the southbound 'Thames–Clyde Express' in May 1959. The train is climbing up the 1-in-100 gradient between Sheffield and Broadway Tunnel, near Millhouses station, which closed in June 1968. After doing the rounds of several sheds— Derby (17A), Saltley (21A) and Burton (17B) — in the early 1960s, this locomotive would be withdawn in October 1963. *Derek Penney*

Title page: Entering the last seven months of its working life, No 45569 *Tasmania* of Leeds Holbeck (55A) lays over at Cricklewood shed (14A) after working a special on 24 September 1963. *Geoff Rixon*

In 1935 the LMS, fired with patriotism (or as a publicity stunt?), decided to commemorate the Silver Jubilee of King George V and Queen Mary by creating a magnificent black-and-silver machine called *Silver Jubilee*. A suitable locomotive would be No 5552, the pioneer of its class, except that it was a bit old (getting on for a year!). Better not to risk it but to use a newer engine and pretend it was No 5552. So the LMS chose No 5642, which entered service in December 1934, to be the first of the class and named it *Silver Jubilee* (see page 4). No 5552 became No 5642, and identities were never changed back. In fact, the substitute No 5552 stayed black right through to 1951.

The exercise turned out to be something of a damp squib. The LMS had chosen, for what was then a rather mediocre engine, the same name that its deadly rival, the LNER, had given to its crack express. Not surprisingly, it was the LNER's 'Silver Jubilee' that the media were more interested in. However, the LMS emerged from the doldrums in 1937 with its celebrated 'Coronation Scot' express.

Following the naming of No 5552, all 'Jubilees' were given names as construction continued through the remainder of 1935 to completion at the end of 1936. The unnamed engines were similarly treated. There were a few random selections, such as *Lord Rutherford of Nelson*: he wasn't at the Battle of Trafalgar — that Nelson was honoured on the preceding engine

First published 2003

ISBN 0 7110 2924 5

© Geoff Rixon 2003

Published by Ian Allan Publishing

an imprint of Ian Allan Publishing Ltd, Hersham, Surrey KT12 4RG.
Printed by Ian Allan Printing Ltd, Hersham, Surrey KT12 4RG.

Code: 0305/B2

— but he did open the LMS Research Laboratory at Rugby! Most of the class were named after countries and states associated with the British Empire. Admirals, naval battles and warships were also commemorated.

In 1942 two 'Jubilees', Nos 5735 and 5736, were rebuilt with larger boilers and were soon reclassified '6P'. It was intended to rebuild the whole class, once the 'Royal Scots' and 'Patriots', which had older boilers, had been dealt with. However, changed circumstances (such as the advent of the Standards) made this unnecessary, and no further 'Jubilees' (and not even all the 'Patriots') were rebuilt.

Apart from the destruction of *Windward Islands* in the horrific Harrow & Wealdstone accident of 1952, the class reached the 1960s intact. The 1950s had witnessed fine performances by 'Jubilees' on the two-hour London–Birmingham expresses but, that apart, they were mainly out of the limelight, carrying out unspectacular and less-demanding duties. Withdrawals arising from creeping dieselisation began in earnest in 1962, but eight much-loved examples lasted into 1967. Some were regularly kept clean by enthusiasts, who replaced their missing nameplates with replica wooden ones, maintaining the survivors' dignity to the last. The 'Jubilees' swansong was hauling summer relief trains over the Settle–Carlisle line. After 33 years of service, the last one, *Alberta*, was withdrawn in November 1967, just months away from the end of main-line steam. Four have escaped destruction: *Kolhapur* and *Bahamas* were purchased for preservation as 'runners', and two more, *Leander* and *Galatea*, were rescued from Barry scrapyard; the latter is incomplete and faces an uncertain future.

My interest in steam locomotives began during World War 2, through having relatives who worked on the railways and obtaining my first Ian Allan spotting book — an LMS one. Itching to start photographing these fine machines, I borrowed my parents' Box Brownie camera, but film was difficult to obtain. I started with ex-RAF reconnaissance film (116 size) purchased from London's Petticoat Lane market. My very first shot of a 'Jubilee', reproduced on this page, was of No 5591 *Udaipur* at Euston on 8 June 1947. It is seen in the short-lived LMS livery that preceded Nationalisation in 1948.

'Jubilees' could be found in most parts of the country and on all Regions, although from September 1964 they were banned from running on the electrified West Coast main line south of Crewe.

In September 1963 regional alterations saw in a number of shed codes changed to reflect the new arrangements. References in this book use the codes current when the photographs were taken.

This book is primarily a pictorial tribute to the 'Jubilees' in their last 12 years of service and is not intended to provide a detailed history of the class. Several books have covered this ground already, and I would recommend, in particular, *LMS Jubilees* by R. J. Essery and G. Toms (published by Wild Swan Publications, 1994) and *Jubilees of the LMS* by John F. Clay (Ian Allan Ltd, 1971). The photographs I have used are the work of several photographers in addition to myself, and without their support this book could not have been published. My grateful thanks go to Gavin Morrison, Derek Penney, Brian Stephenson, T. B. Owen, the late Derek Cross, Brian Magilton, Neville Sims, Alan Tyson, John Edgington, Roy Hobbs and Richard Jelves. Thanks go also to Kevin McCormack, for helping me with the compilation and writing, and to Alan Stokes, for the word-processing.

Geoff Rixon
East Molesey
November 2002

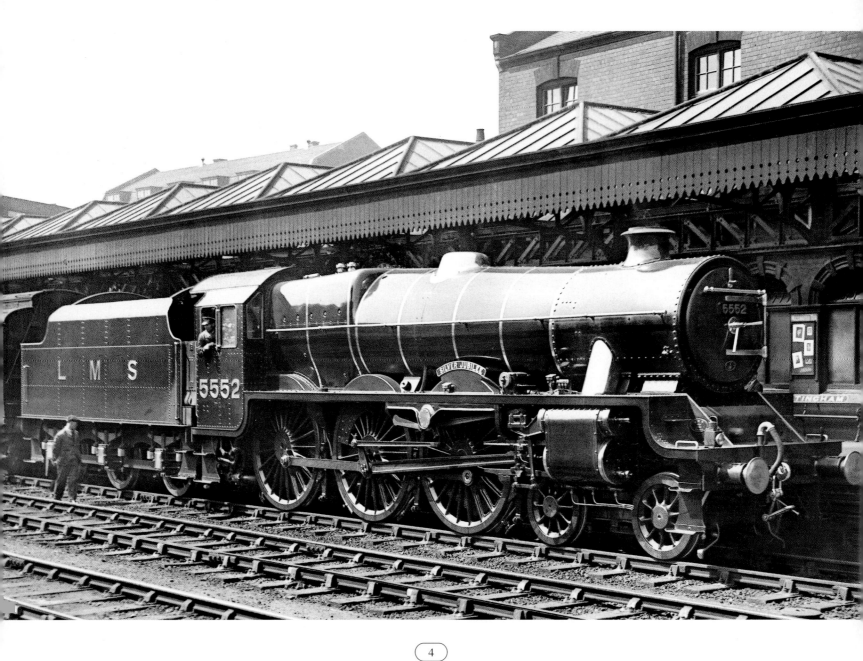

Left: No 5552 *Silver Jubilee,* numerically the first of the 'Jubilee' class, at Nottingham Midland station in 1935, during a tour of the LMS system. *T. G. Hepburn / Rail Archive Stephenson*

Above: Removed from store at Crewe South shed (5B) in 1963 for a final overhaul, the flagship member of the class, No 45552 *Silver Jubilee* leaves Paddington on 6 October 1963 on the

Home Counties Railway Society's Mendips railtour to Bristol. Some of the raised cabside numerals were found to be missing before this trip, and replacements were carefully made from wood. *Silver Jubilee* ended its working life at Crewe North (5A) and was withdrawn in September 1964, sadly not being deemed worthy of preservation. *Geoff Rixon*

Above: Camden (1B)-based 'Jubilee' No 45686 *St. Vincent* hauls a mixed rake of 12 coaches forming a Liverpool–London (Euston) express. The train is passing Hartford, Cheshire, in May 1959. No 45686 was withdrawn from service in November 1962 after transfer to Carnforth shed (24L). *Derek Penney*

Right: Bearing the name of *Mysore*, No 45586 of Aston shed (21D) hauls the 2.25pm from London (Euston) to Walsall in September 1961. The train has just left the tunnel at Kensal Green, some four miles into its journey. *K. L. Cook / Rail Archive Stephenson*

Above: 'Jubilee' No 45603 *Solomon Islands*, based at Nuneaton (2B), has just been turned in Willesden roundhouse in March 1962 and moves off to pick up a duty. Its contented driver grins as he smokes his cigarette. The locomotive was less content, however, being withdrawn just nine months later. *Geoff Rixon*

Right: Getting the most from a locomotive, only weeks before withdrawal, the London Midland Region makes No 45703 *Thunderer* live up to its name by giving it a 13-coach train to haul up Shap. This view shows a Blackpool–Glasgow special at Scout Green on 28 September 1964. The locomotive was transferred in 1964 from Blackpool (10B) to Carnforth (10A), where its service life ended in November of that year. *T. B. Owen*

Above: Looking very neglected, and smoking out the Leeds area, No 45627 *Sierra Leone* pilots Class 5MT No 45336 as it hauls the Heaton–Manchester Red Bank parcels train near Farnley, in April 1966. The 'Jubilee' came from Bank Hall shed (8E) and had only five months to go before withdrawal. *Gavin Morrison*

Right: The silence of an early evening visit to Stafford station is broken by the pounding beat of No 45669 *Fisher,* working a northbound fitted freight on 16 July 1962. The locomotive has been superbly turned out by its home shed, Nuneaton (2B), where it remained until withdrawal in May 1963. *Geoff Rixon*

Left: Until the introduction of the 'Peak' Type 4 diesels in 1961, 'Jubilees' were the mainstay of the Midland main line. Lasting in service until as late as January 1967, No 45565 *Victoria*, a Leeds Holbeck (55A) locomotive, reaches the top of the steep incline out of Sheffield, at Dore & Totley, with a Newcastle–Bristol express, in May 1959. No 45565 moved to Low Moor shed (56F) in early 1962. *Derek Penney*

Above: Ending its days at Llandudno Junction (6G), where it was withdrawn in December 1964, No 45689 *Ajax* was a Crewe North (5A) resident when it was photographed on Bushey water troughs in Hertfordshire on 7 May 1960. The locomotive is hauling a Blackpool train into London (Euston). *T. B. Owen*

Left: Conquering the Lickey Incline with the help of a banker is No 45660 *Rooke.* Seen approaching the summit at Blackwell with a Cardiff–Newcastle train on 11 July 1956, No 45660 was for many years a Bristol Barrow Road (22A) engine. It achieved stardom in 1937 for its hill-climbing abilities on the Settle–Carlisle line, where it produced some remarkable performances on test trains, proving that the 'Jubilees' were supremely capable locomotives. *John Edgington*

Below: Winter sunshine illuminates No 45632 *Tonga,* a Stockport Edgeley (9B) locomotive, as it pulls out of Manchester Exchange in December 1963 with a local train to Wigan. The engine was retired in October 1965; Manchester Exchange closed in May 1969. *Brian Magilton*

Left: Looking decidedly tarnished, the so-called pioneer 'Jubilee', No 45552 *Silver Jubilee*, allocated to Liverpool Edge Hill shed (8A), hauls a Leeds–Liverpool express on 17 May 1960. The train is seen emerging from the tunnel at Lightcliff, near Halifax. Lightcliff station closed in June 1965. *Gavin Morrison*

Above: The sun shines on No 45738 *Samson*, an inappropriately named locomotive for hauling this small parcels train northwards through Etterby Junction, north of Carlisle Citadel station, on 8 September 1962. *Samson* was, at this time, a local 'lad' from Kingmoor (12A) and lasted a further 16 months before his inevitable demise. *Geoff Rixon*

Above: Looking all the better for a good clean and some repainting for an enthusiasts' special, No 45647 *Sturdee* makes an impressive sight working a westbound Leeds–Llandudno parcels train on 10 August 1966. The location is Longwood & Milnsbridge, on the 1-in-105 'Long Drag' between Huddersfield and Marsden. *Gavin Morrison*

Right: Surviving through to 1965, No 45604 *Ceylon* arrives at Colwyn Bay, on the North Wales coast, on 21 July 1964 with a westbound holiday express. Only half of the class was still active at this stage, No 45604 being one of four 'Jubilees' then allocated to Carnforth (10A). *Alan Tyson / Atlantic Publishing*

Above: Ready for a two-hour sprint to Euston is No 45740 *Munster*, seen at Birmingham New Street in September 1956. One of nine 'Jubilees' based at Bushbury, this locomotive was transferred to Carlisle Upperby (12B) in 1960 and then on to neighbouring Carlisle Kingmoor (12A) in 1962, where it remained until withdrawal in 1964. No 45740 was one of the last four 'Jubilees' to be built, named after the four provinces of Ireland. *John Edgington*

Right: Working what is believed to be a Bradford–Poole train in September 1966, No 45562 *Alberta* is seen approaching Millhouses. This locomotive was the longest-serving member of the class but was passed over for preservation, apparently on account of its worn tyres. *Derek Penney*

Above: Here is a view of the famous Ribblehead Viaduct on the Settle–Carlisle line, taken on a perfect summer's day in June 1966. The black smoke comes courtesy of No 45697 *Achilles*, hauling a northbound freight. *Roy Hobbs*

Right: A clean 'Jubilee' on a sunny day is just begging to be photographed — even the crew wanted to get in on the act! No 45595 *Southern Rhodesia*, one of only three of the class to carry badges above the nameplate, prepares to leave Carlisle Upperby shed in September 1962 to pick up a southbound train. The engine was based at Crewe shed and had a lifespan of 30 years, from 1935 to 1965. *Geoff Rixon*

Above: A West Coast main-line express to London (Euston) is photographed near Linslade tunnels in Bedfordshire in the summer of 1962. The train is headed by No 45624 *St. Helena*, which had been on the wander for some time, having no fewer than four different homes in its last few years — Willesden (1A), Chester (6E), Nuneaton (2B) and Manchester Longsight (9A). By November 1963 the engine had run out of sheds and was withdrawn. *Geoff Rixon*

Right: Birmingham-based 'Jubilee' No 45586 *Mysore* of Aston (21D) shed helps out at Euston's No 1 arrival platform on empty-stock duties on 2 March 1963. *Mysore* lasted two more years in service. *Geoff Rixon*

Left: A Midland-line locomotive for nearly all its life and a long-term resident of Leeds Holbeck (55A), No 45639 *Raleigh* heads a Leeds–London (St Pancras) express past Elstree, Hertfordshire. Seen in February 1959, No 45639 was withdrawn in September 1963. *T. B. Owen*

Right: Bristol Barrow Road (82E) has supplied the motive power for this Bristol-bound express, pictured south of Millhouses in May 1959. The locomotive is No 45660 *Rooke*, which finished its days at Leeds Holbeck in June 1966, having been based at Shrewsbury (89A) in the early 1960s. The train depicted here has been diverted from the Midland main line to the Manchester line because of engineering works. *Derek Penney*

Above: No 45649 *Hawkins*, shedded at Burton (17B), hauls a northbound Summer Saturday special over Low Gill, Westmorland, on 1 September 1962. *Gavin Morrison*

Right: No 45591 *Udaipur* reverses towards the roundhouse at Willesden shed to be turned. A Crewe North engine, it was withdrawn four months after this photograph was taken in May 1963. *Geoff Rixon*

Above: No 45661 *Vernon* of Newton Heath (26A), Manchester, leaves Beattock in July 1958 with a Manchester express. The branch line on the right went to Moffat and had closed to passengers in 1954, remaining open for freight. After transfer from Newton Heath in late 1964, the locomotive went to Wakefield (56A) and was withdrawn in May 1965. *K. L. Cook / Rail Archive Stephenson*

Right: A possible 'cop' for the trainspotters at Leeds City in August 1960 is this 'Jubilee', No 45636 *Uganda*. Allocated to Leicester Midland (15C) before going to Burton (17B) and being withdrawn in December 1962, No 45636 has charge of a prestigious working: the up 'Thames–Clyde Express' to London (St Pancras).
Gavin Morrison

Above: A Liverpool–Hull express hauled by No 45646 *Napier* from Stockport Edgeley shed (9B) speeds through the former station at Glazebury which closed on 7 July 1958, a year before this photograph was taken. Allocated to Farnley (55C), No 45646 remained there until withdrawal in December 1963. *Brian Magilton*

Right: Fortunate in receiving an overhaul at Crewe Works so late in its working life, Blackpool (24E)-based No 45653 *Barham* stands at Euston's No 3 arrival platform after working a special from its home town in August 1962. *Barham* was withdrawn in March 1965, after spending its final two years at Newton Heath (9D). *Geoff Rixon*

Left: With only a few days of service left, Leeds Holbeck's No 45675 *Hardy* — one of only three 'Jubilees' still remaining — prepares to leave Bradford (Valley Road) goods depot with a freight for Carlisle on 19 June 1967. *Gavin Morrison*

Right: The Yorkshire Pennines on a fine day in July 1966 as seen through the arches of the Penistone Viaduct, on the former Lancashire & Yorkshire Railway, as No 45647 *Sturdee* passes with a Poole–Bradford parcels train. This locomotive was one of the last surviving members of the class, lingering until April 1967. *Gavin Morrison*

Above: Ominous skies threaten Cumbria on 30 June 1964 as
No 45658 *Keyes* of Leeds Holbeck deputises for a failed diesel
on the up 'Thames–Clyde Express'. With 'Jubilees' decreasing rapidly
in number, this working was a bonus for the photographer.
The location is Kirkby Stephen, on the Settle–Carlisle line.
Alan Tyson / Atlantic Publishing

Right: The interior of London's Camden depot in August 1963, with
the locomotive crews going about their daily duties at the shift office
while Crewe (5A)-based 'Jubilee' No 45554 *Ontario* awaits the call
of duty. The engine had another 15 months of service remaining.
Geoff Rixon

Above: No 45697 *Achilles* works up to Ais Gill Summit in Westmorland with an 11-coach southbound relief 'Thames–Clyde Express' in July 1960. Allocated to Carlisle Kingmoor at this time and paired with a Fowler tender, No 45697 would become one of the last of the class to remain in service, surviving until September 1967. *Gavin Morrison*

Right: For many years a Nottingham (16A)-based engine, No 45611 *Hong Kong* waits at London (St Pancras) to take an express to Leicester in 1960. In 1962 it was relegated to serve at Burton (17B) until withdrawal in September 1964. *Geoff Rixon*

Above: Scotland's last 'Jubilees' were shedded at Glasgow Corkerhill (67A); this view depicts No 45692 *Cyclops* on a Glasgow train at Liverpool Exchange in June 1962. Three months later, all 10 of Corkerhill's 'Jubilees' were put in store; the inset photograph shows sister engine No 45693 *Agamemnon* having its nameplate unbolted by a fitter at Corkerhill in September 1962. *Richard Jelves (main picture), Geoff Rixon*

Far right: One-time resident of Rugby Testing Station (in 1956) No 45722 *Defence* stands outside Derby Works in April 1961 following an intermediate overhaul. The engine then went to Rugby shed (2A) until withdrawal in November 1962. *K. L. Cook / Rail Archive Stephenson*

Above: The second of the two rebuilt 'Jubilees', No 45736 *Phoenix* was a Crewe North engine for many years until 1963, when it moved to Holyhead (6J). It was withdrawn in September 1964, having been transferred to Carlisle Kingmoor (12A). This view shows the locomotive in September 1960, working the up 'Lakes Express' through the London suburb of Kensal Green.
K. L. Cook / Rail Archive Stephenson

Right: As early as 1937 No 45684 *Jutland* was fitted with a Kylchap double blastpipe and chimney. Although enabling it to outperform other members of the class, this modification failed because of excessive spark-throwing and build-up of ash in the smokebox. In this view *Jutland* works a Trent Valley weekday-evening local from Rugby to Stafford, seen leaving Nuneaton on 31 May 1963. The locomotive was withdrawn at Derby (16C) in December 1965. *Neville Sims*

Above: Taking supporters to Wembley on 25 May 1963 for the FA Cup Final betwen Manchester United and Leicester City, No 45622 *Nyasaland* of Burton shed (recently re-coded 16F) puts on a spurt after passing through Rugby station. Just before the outbreak of World War 2 this locomotive recorded the fastest-ever steam run over the Midland main line, covering the 99 miles between Leicester and St Pancras in 84½ minutes. It ended its career 25 years later, in September 1964. *Neville Sims*

Right: One of the two rebuilt 'Jubilees', No 45735 *Comet* stands over the ash-pits at Camden shed (1B) in August 1962. At this stage *Comet* was a Willesden (1A) locomotive and was in fact the only member of its class shedded there in 1962/3. After an unremarkable career working from Annesley (16B) on the former Great Central line, it was withdrawn there in October 1964. *Geoff Rixon*

Left: Passing its home shed of Millhouses (41C) on the Eastern Region, No 45594 *Bhopal* storms out of Sheffield in May 1959. In March 1946 this locomotive had been painted by the LMS in an experimental livery of red with black edging and gold lining. It would be withdrawn in December 1962 at Sheffield Darnall shed (41A). *Derek Penney*

Above: Long-time resident of Crewe North (5A) No 45625 *Sarawak* heads a down express through Beattock in July 1958. The station and shed (68D) are visible in the background. No 45625 moved from Crewe North to Carnforth (24L) in late 1962 and was withdrawn in September 1963. *K. L. Cook / Rail Archive Stephenson*

Left: No 45650 *Blake* spent the whole of its working life on the Midland line. Recently reallocated to Burton (17B), this former Kentish Town (14B) locomotive is seen visiting its old home on 9 June 1962. It was withdrawn seven months later. *Geoff Rixon*

Above: For many years Blackpool shed (24E) had six 'Jubilees' in its care, and these were usually kept in very clean condition. No 45574 *India* was photographed tackling the climb out of Euston, up Camden Bank, in June 1962, at the head of a Blackpool-bound express. The locomotive was withdrawn in March 1966 after a final stint at Leeds Holbeck. *Geoff Rixon*

Left: One of the 50 'Jubilees' built by North British, and one of only five to be renamed during its lifetime, No 45572 *Eire* (*Irish Free State* from 1934 to 1938) simmers at Shrewsbury shed (89A) in June 1962. *Geoff Rixon*

Above: A Manchester Victoria–Glasgow Central express tops Shap Summit, hauled by No 45559 *British Columbia*. Last shedded at Patricroft (26F) and Blackpool (24E), this locomotive became surplus to requirements in October 1962. *Derek Cross*

Above: In the early 1960s Carlisle Kingmoor (12A) had 17 'Jubilees', one of which was No 45728 *Defiance*, seen heading a southbound freight train over Beattock Summit in Dumfries-shire on 4 June 1960. This locomotive survived until September 1962. *Gavin Morrison*

Right: A long-standing resident of Leeds Holbeck (55A) until withdrawal in September 1963, No 45639 *Raleigh* works the down London St Pancras–Glasgow St Enoch 'Thames–Clyde Express' through Wortley Junction, Leeds, on 25 September 1960. *Gavin Morrison*

Left: Another member of the Crewe North brigade of 20 'Jubilees', No 45666 *Cornwallis* works a down parcels train through Nuneaton on 13 September 1963. Electrification of the West Coast main line is well advanced but has yet to come into use. *Cornwallis* would move to Warrington (8B) in 1964, its demise following in March 1965. *Neville Sims*

Above: A view from a convenient road bridge shows No 45562 *Alberta*, the last survivor of the class, hauling a northbound fitted freight out of Finedon Road yard, near Wellingborough, in June 1965. *Alberta* spent the last decade of its working life shedded in the Leeds area, at Farnley (55C) and Holbeck (55A). *Geoff Rixon*

Above: On 25 May 1963 a variety of motive power arrived at Wembley on football specials for the FA Cup Final between Manchester United and Leicester. No 45598 *Basutoland,* turned out in fair condition by its then home shed at Burton (17B), is seen on layover in the carriage siding at Neasden. Having enjoyed spells at Kentish Town (14B) in the 1950s and Derby (17A) in the very early 1960s, *Basutoland* had moved to Burton in the autumn of 1962, remaining until withdrawal in October 1964. *Geoff Rixon*

Right: A 'Jubilee' which lasted until March 1965, No 45602 *British Honduras,* is seen working a holiday special on the North Wales Coast line at Abergele & Pensarn on 14 June 1963. At the time shedded at Newton Heath (9D), the locomotive was transferred to its final home of Wakefield (56A) in 1964. *Geoff Rixon*

Above: The SLS/BLS 'Scottish Easter Rambler' railtour crosses the strengthened Big Fleet Viaduct near Gatehouse of Fleet on 15 April 1963, heading for Stranraer. In charge of the train is No 45588 *Kashmir*. This line from Dumfries was closed in June 1965.
Derek Cross

Right: The final member of the 'Jubilee' class was No 45742 *Connaught*. Between 1946 and 1949 it was fitted with a 2B domed boiler with 28-element superheater and from 1940 to November 1955 sported a double chimney. For many years it was based at Birmingham Bushbury (3B) and worked the two-hour expresses between Birmingham and Euston. Here it is seen arriving at Birmingham New Street in 1956, with the 7.0am Euston–Wolverhampton. By 1961 it had been transferred to Carlisle Upperby (12B), moving to sister shed Carlisle Kingmoor (12A) in the autumn of 1962, where it remained until withdrawn in May 1965. *John Edgington*

Left: This view at York shed (50A) in June 1962 depicts a chance meeting between two locomotives which later dodged the cutter's torch: 'Jubilee' No 45690 *Leander*, an escapee from Barry scrapyard, and 'A4' Pacific No 60007 *Sir Nigel Gresley*. No 45690 was a long-time resident of Bristol Barrow Road (82E) and had probably worked a Bristol–York train. Withdrawn in March 1964, it was extracted from Woodham's scrapyard in 1972 and restored at Derby Works the following year. *Gavin Morrison*

Above: A double-headed Glasgow–Liverpool express is seen at Lamington in Lanarkshire, hauled by No 45664 *Nelson* piloting No 45733 *Novelty* from Millhouses (41E) and Liverpool Edge Hill (8A) sheds respectively. The locomotives will shortly have to face Beattock Summit with their heavy load comprising at least 13 carriages. *Derek Cross*

Above: Viewed from the railway bridge at Brighouse station in Yorkshire during July 1960, No 45717 *Dauntless*, shedded at Bank Hall (27A), calls at the station with a train from Liverpool Exchange to Newcastle. Closed to passengers in January 1970, the station has recently re-opened. *Gavin Morrison*

Right: No 45708 *Resolution* was a Farnley (55C) locomotive from the mid-1950s until withdrawal in February 1964. Here, in the early 1960s, it is seen working a four-coach semi-fast Leeds–Liverpool train, climbing the 1-in-105 gradient at Slaithwaite in Yorkshire, towards Standedge Tunnel. *K. Field / Rail Archive Stephenson*

Above: A Willesden (1A) 'Jubilee', No 45599 *Bechuanaland,* reduced to working a Bletchley–Euston local in August 1960. The train is on the up slow line approaching Hunton Bridge, north of Watford. The locomotive was withdrawn in August 1964, after transfer to Nuneaton (5E). *Geoff Rixon*

Right: There was not much livery visible on Carnforth (24L) 'Jubilee' No 45629 *Straits Settlements* when it made this visit to Carlisle Kingmoor (12A) in September 1963. However, the lack of colour is compensated by the atmosphere created, as it smokes out the entire shed. Eventually No 45629 was reallocated to Kingmoor until withdrawal in March 1965. *Geoff Rixon*

Above: A resident of Carlisle Kingmoor (12A), No 45657 *Tyrwhitt* works hard on the Midland line near Hellifield, with a southbound freight, on a fine October day in 1961. By late 1962 No 45657 had joined three other 'Jubilees' at Bank Hall (27A), where it remained until withdrawal in September 1964. *Gavin Morrison*

Right: With the fireman on point duty, No 45668 *Madden* leaves Willesden (1A) shed yard to take a return Schoolboys' International Football special from Wembley on 27 April 1963. This Burton (17B) engine had only eight months of life remaining. *Geoff Rixon*

Left: This was the final steam-hauled Royal Train until 2002 (which was possibly the last ever). The most remarkable steam working of 1967 occurred on 30 May, when HRH The Duke of Edinburgh visited Nidd Bridge, north of Harrogate. Doing the honours is No 45562 *Alberta*, seen on the former North Eastern line at Wormold Green in Yorkshire. *Gavin Morrison*

Above: The last 'Jubilee' to run with a double blastpipe and chimney, No 45596 *Bahamas*, draws a Manchester-bound freight out of the former LNWR sidings at Copley Hill, Leeds, in April 1965. Shedded at Stockport Edgeley (9B) until withdrawn in July 1966, No 45596 is one of the surviving quartet. *Gavin Morrison*

Above: In May 1966, when only 10 'Jubilees' (out of 191) remained in service, No 45565 *Victoria* works a Leeds–Blackpool excursion through the Calder Valley. The train is seen leaving Horsfall Tunnel, northeast of Todmorden. In 1948 *Victoria* had been outshopped in an experimental livery of very light green with orange-and-white lining. *Roy Hobbs*

Right: Hillmorton in Warwickshire, on the former LNWR line near Rugby, was the location chosen to photograph Crewe North (5A) 'Jubilee' No 45554 *Ontario*. The locomotive is seen working a South Coast–West Midlands special on 17 August 1963. *Neville Sims*

Left: Outshopped from Crewe Works in 1961 with double blastpipe and chimney, No 45596 *Bahamas* simmers at its home shed of Stockport (9B) in May 1966. Withdrawn two months later, this locomotive has continued its working life in preservation. *Derek Penney*

Above: Carnforth-based 'Jubilee' No 45696 *Arethusa* stands on the turntable at its home shed on 8 September 1962, attached to a Fowler tender. These were being phased out on 'Jubilees' around this time. The large cabside numerals were a trademark of St Rollox Works in Glasgow, where this locomotive was overhauled. *Arethusa* was withdrawn in July 1964. *Geoff Rixon*

Above: Bristol had its own fair share of 'Jubilees', but when photographed at Temple Meads at the head of a Birmingham-bound express in September 1961 No 45626 *Seychelles* was a Derby (17A) engine. By 1962 Derby's nine 'Jubilees' had been transferred to Burton (17B); after a subsequent spell at Leeds (55A), No 45626 was withdrawn in October 1965. *M. J. Fox / Rail Archive Stephenson*

Right: No 45577 *Bengal* waits to reverse onto its Birkenhead-bound train at Shrewsbury in June 1963. Shrewsbury (89A) was a Western Region shed at this time but became a London Midland Region shed (6D) later in the year. No 45577 remained at Shrewsbury shed until withdrawal in September 1964. *Derek Penney*

Above: One of the preserved 'Jubilees', No 5690 *Leander*, piloted by the National Railway Museum's Midland 4-4-0 Compound No 1000, works a special on the Settle–Carlisle line on 12 February 1983. This chilly scene is near Langwathby, 20 miles south of Carlisle.
Geoff Rixon

Right: Storming towards preservation with three months to go, No 45593 *Kolhapur* hauls a Saturdays-only Leeds–Llandudno express through Longwood, near Huddersfield, on 8 July 1967.
Gavin Morrison

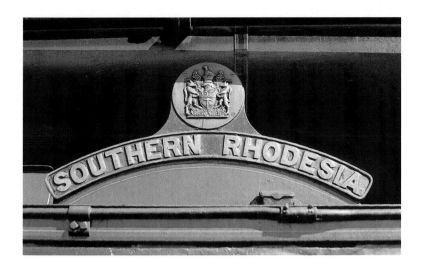

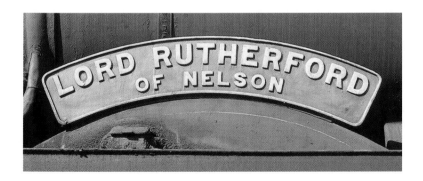

Above left and above: Only three members of the 'Jubilee' class carried badges with their nameplates, those of No 45595 *Southern Rhodesia* and No 45706 *Express* being shown. The other was No 45739 *Ulster*. *Geoff Rixon*

Below left: Just two members of the class carried double-line nameplates, that of No 45665 *Lord Rutherford of Nelson* being shown here. The other was No 45609 *Gilbert and Ellice Islands*. *Geoff Rixon*

Below: For comparison, No 45670 *Howard of Effingham* shows its long name on a normal plate. *Geoff Rixon*

Left: With Park Fell in the background, a forlorn-looking No 45618 *New Hebrides* stops for water in the bleak surroundings of Blea Moor on the Settle–Carlisle line while hauling a freight in March 1962. Allocated at that time to Derby (17A) this engine was transferred to Burton (17B) later in the year, remaining in service until February 1964. *Alan Tyson / Atlantic Publishing*

Index of Locations

Back cover: The Schoolboys' International day at Wembley was guaranteed to bring many visiting engines to Willesden shed (1A), and 27 April 1963 was no exception. Here is No 45590 *Travancore* of Agecroft shed (26B) reversing into Willesden motive-power depot. By 1964 the locomotive had been transferred to Warrington (8B), from where it was withdrawn in December 1965. *Geoff Rixon*